INSTRUMENTS OF POPULAR MUSIC

Uillean pipes

A History of Musical Instruments

INSTRUMENTS

OF

POPULAR MUSIC

LILLA M. FOX

with drawings by the author

ROY PUBLISHERS, INC.
NEW YORK 10021

FOR MY MOTHER

Acknowledgements

I would like to acknowledge the help I have received from the staff of the Horniman Museum and Library, of the English Folk Dance and Song Society and the Vaughan Williams Memorial Library, of the Victoria and Albert Museum and the Reigate and Redhill Public Libraries. My especial thanks are due to Jeremy Montague of the Galpin Society and Peter Kennedy of the English Folk Dance and Song Society for their invaluable help and advice.

L.M.F.

Library of Congress Catalog Card No. 68–13294

Printed in Great Britain

Contents

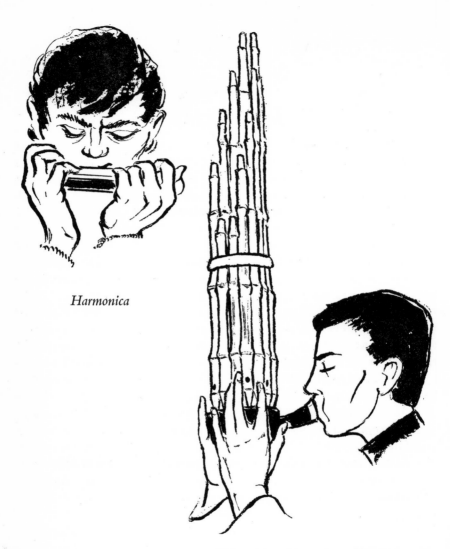

Harmonica

Chinese mouth organ, or Cheng

Introduction

NOWADAYS ANYONE can listen to anything: we can buy a record of any instrument from a harmonica to a Chinese Cheng, or listen to a beat group or a classical orchestra in our own rooms. It is easy to forget that only sixty years ago, even those few who had one of the new phonographs had nothing like the same listening experience. Over half the population lived in the towns and had little money to spare; they might hear little more than the organ in church, the piano down at the local, and the band in the park on Sunday. It is not surprising that small children got lost wandering after street musicians, brass band parades, or the Salvation Army with their concertinas and tambourines.

A hundred years before that, these sounds were unknown. The town dweller had the chance to hear a concert in the Gardens now and then, or a good military band—not as we know it, but one with trumpets, serpent, hautboys, clarinets, bassoons, horns, and an assortment of percussion. But the country people, then the bulk of the population, had only their own music and that of travelling minstrels to listen to. Many country churches had bands with fiddles, violas da gamba, flutes, oboes, bassoons, and sometimes a serpent or a clarinet; often the players made their own instruments, and played for dancing and singing in the village. People sang and danced to the old instruments that their ancestors had heard before them, hundreds of years ago: the bagpipes, the shrill pipe played with a tabor for rhythm, the crowd and rebec, and probably the oldest of all, the hornpipe and the harp.

There were, of course, other instruments. The medieval Waits, who were watchmen on the city walls, had drums, horns and pipes, on which to sound the hour or the alarm; they played for processions and feasts,

Fifteenth-century morris dancers with pipe and tabor

and as the centuries passed, became town bands, adding serpent, haut-boy, bassoon and sackbut, and finally the full brass. The army marched to fife and drum before the days of Elizabeth I. The horn was heard at the hunt, on the battlefield, and calling up the herds. The Court and nobles had their own minstrels who played such instruments as the lute, gittern, fydel, psaltery, and shawm, and, for those of the blood royal, the trumpet and kettle-drums; other household servants could hear all this, and servants in later centuries were often expected to bear a part in their master's music.

This book is concerned with instruments played by the ordinary people of this country for their own enjoyment. At the present time, this would make a formidable list, since any one, given the will and ability, can learn to play any instrument he likes; people play in orchestras, string ensembles, brass and pipe bands, and jazz, folk and pop groups. To cover all the instruments and their various uses would take many volumes; therefore, any part they may play in orchestral or processional music, or music connected with magic or religion, can only be mentioned in passing.

Before the days of large concert halls, recorded music or radio, most of our ancestors heard little besides music in church and their own folk music. They also heard popular airs, sung, or sold when printing became cheap; these were often derived from folk airs, and many have become once more part of the stream of folk music. Folk music started with song: song to tell a story, to accompany ritual dance, and to express the feelings of the people amongst whom it was sung. (Most instruments played for folk music allow the player to sing as well.)

Rooted in human life and experience, it is enduring, and handed down from one generation to another. It changes with circumstances as when, in the early years of the Industrial Age, new songs arose from new conditions. Later, with the break-up of village life and the crowded poverty-stricken existence of the new towns, folk music was almost lost. Fortunately, folk revivalists sought it out where it still survived, and saved all they could; there are still folk musicians in remote places who carry on a living tradition, while from time to time, new singers arise, ordinary men and women with the gift for expressing in word and music the

The English harp of early medieval times

The psaltery

aspirations, the fears, and the complicated emotional temper of their own time and generation.

Popular song, from yesterday's hit to the ballads hawked in Queen Anne's London and the earlier songs of wandering minstrels, was always intended to catch the fancy for a short time and then to give way to the

Folk singer with button-key accordion

Seventeenth-century fiddle played for dancing (after Playford)

next. The same is true of music-hall songs, pub songs, and the catches or rounds that were so popular in Tudor times and earlier. Some of these have lasted, and are still heard in pubs, or have become nursery rhymes or national songs. We cannot know how many airs are lost and forgotten or, wandering around in our collective memory of music, appear and reappear in new songs and new dances.

The instruments described here will have been used to accompany singing and dancing and the every-day music of the people. Some may seem to receive short shrift; that is because their main place has been in the orchestra, the consort, or the band, and they will be more fully dealt with in the future.

Folk singer's twelve-string guitar

1   THE GUITAR—I

THE GUITAR IS ONE of the most popular of all instruments; there are concert and folk guitarists, and pop players who depend on electrical amplification for tone and volume and have a variety of differently shaped instruments. (It is not the first time that other versions of the guitar have been made.)

To understand how guitar playing has become so widespread, one has to look back to the colonization of the Americas when European immigrants brought with them their folk music and instruments; among the earliest was the guitar from Spain and Portugal where it had been played for over five hundred years. In the nineteenth century, it was a drawing-room instrument in Europe, and as such also was taken across the Atlantic. In the United States, where some European folk music has lived on and new folk traditions have arisen, the guitar has become its most frequent accompaniment. Lone cowboys played it on the ranges; wandering singers played it in saloons and barrel-houses and singing along the streets; Negroes called it Easy Rider or See See Rider, a countryside name for a woman; in the double meaning of solace in loneliness and the desired lover, it is associated with many of the old classic blues. Some of the early blues players made guitars with metal soundtables and without frets, and, laying them across their knees, slid a bottle neck or a steel tube up and down the finger-board. The smaller Hawaiian guitar, developed from the Portuguese guitar, the machete, which travelled there via the Philippines, is also played with a sliding steel, the *glissando* being part of the distinctive whining sound of these instruments. Shetland folk players, too, use the steel, and play chordal accompaniments to their songs; it is possible that in their case the "across the knees" playing may be inherited from the playing of older Nordic instruments. (See Appalachian or Mountain Dulcimer.)

Skiffle group of the fifties

The guitar was, and is, played in ragtime, jazz, blues, country and western, and skiffle; these movements, and pop based on them, became known here, and their instrumental techniques adopted. Skiffle has contributed more than any to the popularity of the guitar. Skiffle originally meant any sort of impromptu music, using jugs, lead piping, washboards, and whatever came to hand, often with a guitar or banjo as lead instrument. About the turn of the century there were "spasm" or skiffle bands with a strong jazz spirit playing in New Orleans streets; later, skiffle bands went to rent-collecting parties in the poor quarters of Chicago. In the twenties, there were some commercial skiffle groups, or Blue Blowers, where the lead was supplied by comb and paper or kazoos accompanied by various combinations of washboard, string bass, jug, banjo, clarinet or guitar. Blue Blowing was revived in the forties; it

The ukelele   *Small-size guitar*

came here, bringing with it the folk songs of the New World. In the late fifties, the English form of skiffle (folk or pop songs accompanied by open string guitars, washboard, and tea-chest bass,) caught the mood of the times; all over the country, young men formed skiffle groups, playing wherever their audience could gather round to listen.

Since then, we have seen a new revival of folk music, and the growth of music-making, both individual and in groups. The guitar, whether the six- or twelve-string folk guitar or the electric, is the chief instrument and many people have learned to play it.

13

Before the last war, the guitar was chiefly a concert instrument. There were guitarists in some jazz bands and gypsy bands; but for popular music in pierrot shows, music-halls, informal parties in pubs, etc., the banjo and the ukelele were most often heard. The ukelele, still played by some pop players, is a small four-stringed guitar which provides simple chord accompaniments; it is thought to have developed from the Portuguese machete. The mandoline was also fairly popular; both it and the guitar had been, off and on, drawing-room instruments since the eighteenth century; drawing-room music had declined with the coming of the gramophone, but before then generations of young ladies had sung genteel if flowery and sentimental songs to these instruments. At one period, small size, short-necked guitars were made for the "weaker sex" —not in this case the legions of working-class girls who were engaged on anything from chain-forging to sweated lace-making, and had little time to hear, let alone play, any musical instrument.

It was at the beginning of the nineteenth century that the guitar was taken up as a concert rather than a chamber music instrument: it had a

Lyre guitar, twelve-stringed guitar, and harp guitar

Eighteenth-century guitar and mandoline

wave of popularity in musical circles, and there was a fashion for different versions. The French Revolution had broken conventions binding the arts: there was a new spirit abroad, and also a craze for the Classical. Enthusiasts made harp guitars, lyre guitars, and even double harp guitars (all now museum pieces) with the intention of combining the romantic sound of the harp with the simpler technique and smaller size of the guitar, and giving the whole instrument a suitably Classical appearance.

By the end of the eighteenth century the guitar was established in its present-day form, with six gut strings, and a clear mellow tone. Earlier guitars were narrower and less waisted, and usually had five pairs of strings. During the eighteenth century, and until the classical revival, it declined in popularity, while the aristocratic lute (now happily revived) died out.

Lutes in various forms are played all over the world. The European lute came from the Middle East in the late thirteenth century; it is made of thinnest wood; the rose, or soundhole, is often carved, and the instrument is so light and exquisitely made that it sounds to the lightest touch. As with many keyboard instruments, the lightness and responsiveness of the woods with which it is made is all-important; a lute made entirely of gold, and one of ivory, were no use at all. The six pairs of gut strings are difficult to tune, and the catgut frets are tied by the player, the placing requiring much skill: it is not easy to play, but rewards the diligent player with its powers of expression and silvery tone. Before the development of the viol and violin families and the guitar in its newer form, the lute had been the best known of all stringed instruments and a great deal of music was written for it.

The mandoline was introduced from Italy during the eighteenth century. It is a small lute-shaped instrument; the earlier Milanese mandoline had gut strings and was finger played, while the later Neapolitan instrument had four pairs of wire strings and was played with a plectrum in such a way as to produce the distinctive tremulo; this is the form in which it is generally played here. Simpler to play than the lute, it quickly became popular. These fretted instruments, apart from any place they might have in operatic or orchestral music of the eighteenth century, were played by the wealthy and educated.

Not that the ordinary people were unmusical: folk music was very much alive, as were the lighter catches, or rounds, and the topical ballads. Townsmen sang popular airs to the so-called English guitar, which was in reality a revival of the earlier cittern; it had five pairs of metal strings, and, simply played with fingers or plectrum, it sounded bright and crisp, and was a great favourite.

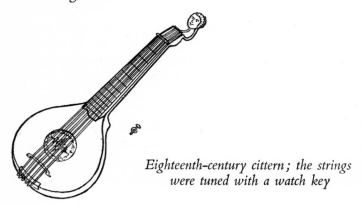

Eighteenth-century cittern; the strings
were tuned with a watch key

Cittern, pandora and opharion, early seventeenth century

2 THE GUITAR—II

"THE FINE EASIE GHITTAR, whose performance is soon gained, at least after the brushing way, hath at this present over top't the nobler lute." So wrote William Turner, singer and composer, in 1690, at a time when gentlemen were not always as assiduous in the pursuit of serious music as had been their fathers, and some of them took to instruments that could sound well with only a little skill or practice. As we know from present experience, the guitar is one of these.

Nevertheless, music was still very much a part of the life of seventeenth-century gentlefolk; Pepys constantly refers to formal and informal music parties, to concerts, and to music in the Gardens, such as Vauxhall, which provided so much of London's entertainment. Their dignified mansions housed musical instruments, and in workshops skilled crafts-men were ever improving on the construction of string and wind in-strument alike. As well as the lute and guitar, gentlemen played the cittern and other wire-strung flat-backed instruments, such as the Opharion, and the pandora: these were consort instruments, used to provide higher or lower parts to lute or cittern, and to take part in a "broken" or mixed consort of instruments. (The consort was an instrumental group based on the vocal group of soprano, alto, tenor, and bass, usually different sizes of the same instrument; consort players could, and often did, play from music scored for voices.)

The cittern was also popular among the people, and was known as the barbers' shop instrument. The barber, who also performed some of the

Elizabethan barber's shop music, with guitar and cittern

services of doctor and dentist, had a large clientele, and he or one of them might entertain the company with a song to the cittern. Another customer would also pick up an instrument—there was often a guitar as well, and in Elizabethan times sometimes a virginal—and others would supply a beat with whatever came handy. Barbers' music came to mean any sort of noisy extempore music-making. Pepys describes how, on board ship, the Admiral "called for the lieutenant's cittern, and with the aid of two candlesticks with money in them, for symbols, we made barbers' music, with which my Lord was well pleased".

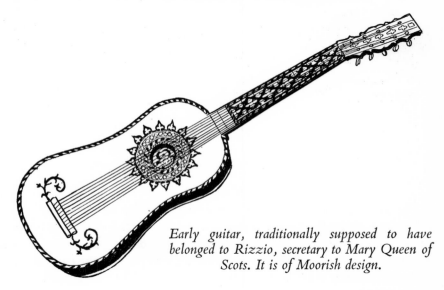

Early guitar, traditionally supposed to have belonged to Rizzio, secretary to Mary Queen of Scots. It is of Moorish design.

In the later years of Elizabeth I, royalty and nobles had their own musicians, and educated people were expected to play an instrument and bear a part in singing: servants were often chosen for their musical ability, and were taught to take their part. Folk music flourished, and it has been said that, at this time, the music of the court and of the people was closer than at any other time, and that England was "a nest of singing birds".

Seventeenth-century lute, chitarrone and theorbo

The lute was the most played of stringed instruments, and in the later part of the sixteenth century, European luthiers were building archlutes with a longer length and depth of tone and still longer bass strings to be plucked unstopped by the fingers. These were to provide the bass for the consorts. Among them were the theorbo, and the larger chitarrone with bass strings over five feet long.

Improved instruments from Spain, called guitars or Spanish Vialles, had been brought to the English court even before Mary Tudor married Philip of Spain. They were smaller than later guitars, with a shorter scale length, and some had slightly curved backs; many were decorated with inlay of ivory and mother-of-pearl, and the roses filled with a filigree of delicate carving. The number and doubling of the strings varied, the earlier models usually four course, with double strings, and the later, five course. In 1554 a young nobleman, Thomas Whytehorne, wrote: "A gittern I then yused to play on very often, yea, and almost every hour of the day, for that it was an instrument much esteemed and yused of gentilmen and of the best sort in those days." John Laneham, a servant of the Queen's, wrote about his amusements: "Sometimes I foot it with dancing; now with my gittern, and else with my cittern; then at the virginals (you know nothing ever comes amiss to me); then carol I up a song withal." (This young man reeived swift promotion!)

Meanwhile, at about the same time, one John Felde "did absent himself from his master his service and went running about the country with a gittern". The merchants of Newcastle, in a long list of complaints about their apprentices, cited "the use of gitterns by night".

Fifteenth-century gittern

The nobleman's gittern may well have been the new Spanish Vialle, while the apprentices and the runaway probably played the old gittern which continued to be popular in England during the sixteenth century. This was a durable instrument, the body and neck being cut from one piece of wood, and often ornately carved; sometimes the head, carved to represent an animal, curved back on to the neck, leaving a gap for the player's fingers. An existing gittern, dated about 1330, was given to Queen Elizabeth by the Earl of Leicester, probably more as a curiosity than an instrument to play.

Versions of the medieval cithole (cittern) and gittern, based on the Exeter Cathedral Minstrels. Both were played with a plectrum

The gittern was held horizontally and played with a plectrum; it can be seen in medieval carvings and manuscripts, together with the cittern, then called cithole or sistole, and the lute. The lute was then a smaller instrument, with four strings, played with a quill or plectrum; it was the chief instrument played by minstrels attached to noble houses, and is associated with the lyrical music of troubadour and trouvière, especially their love songs.

The poorer and the travelling minstrels took with them the cithole and the gittern. The cithole was also played by higher minstrels, as witness the many Italian pictures where it is played by angels; it may have developed from the Spanish oval fiddle; in the Victoria and Albert Museum a replica of a twelfth-century Spanish arch shows these both bowed and plucked. On the other hand, the scrolls at the shoulders of cittern and gittern suggest that both may have developed from ancient stringed instruments, pictured in the Utrecht Psalter of about A.D. 860. The shape of these suggests that they may have developed from the more ancient lyre, being in effect lyres with finger-boards and consequently fewer strings, with the wings shrunk to part of the sound-box.

Stringed instruments from the Utrecht psalter, dating from A.D. 860 and possibly older

Five-string folk banjo

Modern jazz banjo

3

THE BANJO HAS ALWAYS been a jazz and folk instrument in America, and the recent folk revival has brought back to this country the five-string finger-played banjo. For some jazz, and in the large pre-war jazz ensembles and dance bands, the plectrum-played banjo was played; there were different models, with varying number of strings, and often metal resonators for extra volume. It is this type of banjo, with its loud metallic plinketty-plonk, as opposed to the twanging of the guitar and tremulo of the mandoline with which it was often teamed, that was for so long a favourite instrument in concert troupes and music-halls. It needed no mike (being played before that was even heard of) and its sound could carry along the beach or fill a hall. At the same time it was bought by many young men to be played for enjoyment and whenever an accompaniment was wanted for a sing-song. Readers will remember how H. G. Wells's Kipps, living in as a poorly-paid draper's assistant, longed for a banjo; it was the first thing he bought when he suddenly became rich.

It had a brief interlude with the young ladies in the drawing-rooms of the 1890's, but for the most part it was an instrument for working-class young men and girls, filling, perhaps, the gap left by the cittern. It went with soldiers into unknown and unfriendly territory overseas. Ignoring the rich and complex instrumental music of Africa, India and the Far East, Kipling wrote:

"There was never voice before us till I led our lonely chorus,
I, the war drum of the white man round the world."
(*Song of the Banjo*)

He also paid tribute to its hardiness ("I travel with the cooking pots and pails . . .") and its powers of poignant evocation of home.

Long before jazz and ragtime, the banjo came here with the white "Nigger Minstrels". These have had a recent and sophisticated revival; there were minstrel troupes playing in town and seaside theatres in the twenties, but their great days were before the First World War. They had a song and dance routine, interspersed with patter in a dialect supposedly that of the plantation Negro. The first in this country were street players of the mid-nineteenth century, entertainers always on the lookout for new types of show. To quote from a reply made by one of them to Henry Mayhew: "Some Niggers are Irish. There's Scotch Niggers too. I don't know a Welsh one, but one of the street singers is a real black—an African."

Their instruments were bones, tambourine and banjo. "It's hard to play the bones well; it brings the skin off . . . the banjo is the hardest to learn of the lot."

Nigger Minstrels came from America, where they had been started by a white entertainer with a song and dance called "Jim Crow". From 1830 onwards, this became a craze on both sides of the Atlantic; shops were filled with Jim Crow novelties, and one after another, Nigger troupes sprang up, notably the Christy and Kentucky Minstrels. They sang a series of Coon songs which presented the Negro as a simple and comic being, much devoted to his Massa and the ole plantation; a conception acceptable to the white population, and as far from the real Negro people as were the sentimental songs from jazz and the blues.

Mid-nineteenth-century Nigger Minstrels or "Ethiopian Serenaders", from Henry Mayhew's London Labour and the London Poor, 1851

However, the banjo was played on the plantations as early as the eighteenth century—although that was late in the history of slavery which had started in 1619, and ended in 1864, a good thirty years after the birth of the Jim Crow travesty. Sometimes known as the "banger" or the "bonjo", it was at first home made, and its tambour-like open back, and skin or parchment belly suggest that the idea came from Africa where there are some open-back skin-belly lutes in use. The conditions under which Negroes were rounded up and shipped over the Atlantic did not allow them to bring personal possessions, not even the drums which are so important to African music and ritual. Many slaveowners forbade the making or playing of drums since they feared conspiracy among the slaves; there are stories of muffled drums being beaten in secret.

When it was possible for the slaves to have some sort of life of their own, they obtained or made any instrument they could. It was, then, possible that the memory of a homeland instrument could be translated into a present reality, using the materials that came to hand, such as primitive tambours, or household things like sieves.

Home-made plantation banjo

Together, they played before admiring relatives

4   THE VIOL AND VIOLIN FAMILIES—I

FEW PEOPLE TAKE UP the violin in these days, unless they intend to become serious musicians. One of the most expressive instruments, it is also one of the most difficult to master, needing much practice. Bowing technique is difficult, and there are no frets on the finger-board. "My fingers never seemed to be in the right places" wrote the artist E. H. Shepherd about his childhood experiences with the violin, and any of the small boys sent out to music lessons before the war and in Victorian times would know just what he meant. It was more often the boys who learned the violin, while the girls learned the piano; together, they played before admiring relatives. Some of the youthful performers might become professional musicians; others kept up their music for love of it.

The nineteenth century was a great time for drawing-room music as well as concerts, and the showy compositions of the period allowed the enthusiastic amateur to revel in *glissando* and *vibrato*. Indeed, when he played *obbligato* to an equally enthusiastic singer, the result might well drive the audience to tears!

At the same time, there were children of the poor born into the tradition of folk fiddling; there are still folk fiddlers, especially in remote parts of Ireland and Scotland, and there used to be many more. They were working people who played for singing and dancing, or itinerant players. Folk players adapt any instrument to their own use, and, as first the medieval fydel or fythule—to quote two of many spellings—and later the violin came into their hands, a complex technique was handed down

Folk fiddler playing for Bamford Morris Dances

the generations. It is not rigid; the player plays as best suits him. He tunes the fiddle in fourths or fifths—the latter is the conventional tuning; he usually plays an open string as a bourdon, as in Scottish reels; he holds the fiddle in various ways, some of which enable him to sing as well as play. Some of these techniques hark back as far as the complicated rules laid down for thirteenth-century minstrels.

Nineteenth-century ship's fiddler

The fiddle was also played by the city street musicians who were always on the look out for the latest air or ballad; it is still played by buskers. Many of the old sailing vessels had a fiddler, and so important was he to life at sea that the Navy included fiddlers in their ships' companies.

The violin family, violin, viola, cello and double bass, were played a great deal in both the private music parties of the eighteenth century and the newly popular opera, ballet and public concerts. (With the increase of public music, however, many gentlemen felt that the actual playing was the business of hired musicians who, however gifted and cultured they might be, were inferiors.) The construction of the violin had been perfected in the late seventeenth century by the craftsmen families of Italy, among whom Stradivarius is the most famous name. It became established here during that time: Samuel Pepys, ever ready to try out a new instrument, wrote of his "viallin". Gradually, as it improved in construction and performance, the violin family took the place of the viol family. The viols had been played for serious music while the violin was only an instrument for rustic dance and song. They are not, as some people say, an early form of violin, but a family in their own right; they

Seventeenth-century treble and tenor viols, and viola da gamba

are deeper than violins, have flat backs, six strings, fretted finger-boards, the gut frets being tied by hand as on the lute, and a very slightly arched bridge which enables the player to play two or three strings at a time. Their tone is less full and rich than that of the violin family, but is well suited to the music of its time which was more exact and less dramatic than that of the late eighteenth and nineteenth centuries.

A Chest of viols, necessary to any noble or wealthy family, was a consort suitable for family playing, and might consist of two treble or descant viols, two tenors, and two basses. The bass viol or viola da gamba,

31

for which English players were famous, outlasted the other viols, although the musician and historian Dr. Charles Burney wrote that its tones were "so crude and nasal that nothing but the greatest skill . . . can make them bearable"; it found its way into some village church bands, and thence to country dance music. The double bass owes much to the viol family: the first were too large and cumbersome, so later ones were modelled on the violone, the double bass viol. The viola d'amore is partly like a violin, being fretless and played at the shoulder, but has a viol shape; it has sympathetic wire strings running beneath the bowed strings, which give it a romantic singing sound. The viol family has been revived, and can be heard on record and radio.

Folk and travelling fiddlers, playing at fairs, in taverns, and on village greens, were a common feature of town and countryside. In Wales, the fiddler or harpist was sometimes accompanied by a crwth (crowd), descendant of an ancient instrument, which provided a tenor part, and had two bourdon strings, usually plucked by the left thumb. Occasionally fiddlers played the kit, a pocket fiddle sometimes shaped like a small

Eighteenth-century viola d'amore. Note the sympathetic strings running through the bridge and under the fingerboard to the pegs

fiddle and sometimes long and narrow with a rounded end. It was commonly known as the dancing master's instrument, enabling him to play as well as demonstrate the steps.

Pre-Restoration gentlemen, who took their music seriously, "esteemed a violin to be an instrument only belonging to a common fiddler, and could not endure that it should come among them, for feare of making their meetings to be vain and fiddling". So wrote Anthony Wood,

The crwth or crowd

an antiquarian of that time; while Thomas Mace, in his *Musick's Monument* of 1676: wrote: "Scoulding violins be fit to make a Man's Ears Glow, and to fill his brains full of Friskes (dances) . . . than to Sober his Mind and Elevate his Affections to Goodness . . ." Undoubtedly the violin of those days was shrill and squeaky; Playford, however, called it "cheerful and spritely", qualities which made it more suitable for dance music than the gentler viol. (The Playfords, father and son, were music

c

The dancing-master's kit fiddle

publishers in the second half of the seventeenth century; they brought out not only music, but dancing manuals and tutors for all the instruments of their time.)

The violin, like the bagpipe, was played for dancing and revelry, often, in the country, with the "jocund rebec" (Milton), and the crowd, then not only played in Wales; the name "crowder" was applied to the player of any of these instruments. The rebec was a tough instrument, the neck and body cut from one block of wood; it may have played the leading part, the violin the descant, and the deeper crowd the tenor.

This, then, was the music our ancestors danced and sang to on holidays, and on Sundays after church—their only free time. It is incorrect that music and dancing were forbidden during the Commonwealth period;

in fact, Playford published the first issue of his famous manual *The Dancing Master* in 1650 (see p. 10); John Bunyan, a metal worker by trade, made himself a steel fiddle; Milton was a musician; Cromwell encouraged the playing of good music. Much Church music was banned— that is another story—and the playhouses were closed, thus depriving the townsfolk of a source of topical catches and bawdy ballads. Masques, plays, and music went on in the houses of the wealthy, and there were music clubs amongst the merchants, master craftsmen and tradesmen, scholars and the like; it was partly due to the interest of such men that so much instrumental experiment and development took place. Music and its instruments shared in the practical interest in science that was a characteristic of the period.

A strong Puritan tide had been running since the Reformation. Sunday dancing had actually been forbidden by law for some years at the end

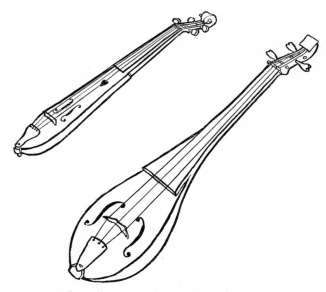

Eighteenth-century kit, and an older rebec

of Elizabeth's reign. But such a law would be very hard to enforce in every village and hamlet at a time when these places were far more isolated than they are now; doubtless there were some parts of the country where Puritan feeling among the majority stopped the old revels, while in other parts life carried on much as usual. There must have been other Puritans like the Elizabethan Dick Harvey, who "having preacht and beat down three pulpits in inveighing against dauncing, one Sunday evening when his wench or friskin was footing it alofte on the green, with foote out and foote in . . . he came sneaking behind a tree and lookt on, though he was loth to countenance the sport, having laid God's word against it so dreadfully; yet to show his good will to it in his heart, hee sent her eighteen pence in hugger-mugger, to pay the fiddlers".

Fiddles and rebec played for country dancing in the sixteenth century

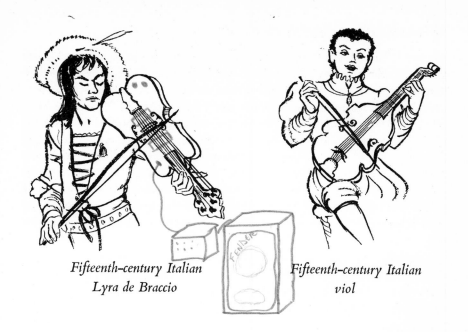

*Fifteenth-century Italian
Lyra de Braccio*

*Fifteenth-century Italian
viol*

5   THE VIOL AND VIOLIN FAMILIES—II

THE LUTHIERS OF ITALY, the most skilled of their craft, in the sixteenth century developed the violin from the earlier Lyra de Braccio;
this was played at the shoulder (de braccio means "of the arm") and
had bourdon strings to be plucked by the left thumb. The viol family
was developed from the Spanish vihuela, a large guitar-type instrument
with a curved back; the first was the viola da gamba, meaning the viol
played on or against the leg. Italian and Flemish pictures of this period
show many different versions of these instruments, and bear witness to
the great amount of experiment made by craftsmen and musicians. The
cities of Flanders and the Western German states and Italy were full of
music; it was not until later in the century that it became part of the life
and education of Tudor gentlefolk here, and the nation became musical
in a way not equalled since. Many instruments, such as the recorder, were

played in Whole Consort—that is, different sizes of the same instrument to play different parts of the music—or in Broken Consort, when other instruments played certain parts. Virginals, cittern, lute, and gittern were popular, and we read of a wedding party who brought "Harpes, Lutes, Kyttes, Basens, and Drommes, wherewith they troubled the whole church". Rebec, fiddle, and crowd, as well as bagpipes, were played by folk musicians. It is, however, difficult to find out about early folk music; chroniclers did not think that "rustic" music was worth writing about; with the exception of certain folk-song collectors—Samuel Pepys was one—it was not until the end of the last century that musicians took it seriously and started to collect what survived of a once rich heritage.

Gentlemen played only amongst themselves; they would lose esteem if beheld "in the similitude of a common servant or minstrel"; minstrels were servants, even the King's Players. However, those attached to the Court and nobility, or to the larger towns, were important people and entitled to wear gorgeous liveries: they were jealous of their good name, and in the sixteenth and fifteenth centuries their Guilds were powerful bodies. In 1469 the Minstrels Charter of Incorporation gave them power to "examine the pretensions of all who exercised the minstrels' profession, to regulate, govern, and punish". They had apprentices, to whom they passed on the skills and secrets of their profession. There were also wandering players, many of whom were outside the control or the protection of the Guilds, and were, like other wandering entertainers such as tumblers, mountebanks, and men with dancing bears, often called rogues and vagabonds with good reason.

Before the establishment of the Guilds, a process which took some time, there were in addition to household, Court and Church musicians many of these wandering players and singers; in 1381 a Rex Minstrelorum, or Minstrels' Governor, was appointed to try to keep some order among them all. The aristocrats of the Minstrel profession were the troubadours who attended their masters at home and on the battlefield; it was they who composed much medieval music, and they had assistants who had to be skilled in many forms of entertainment. These jongleurs—the word

38

means musical entertainer—travelled, and had entrance to noble house-holds where they not only entertained but carried news and sometimes secret messages.

The Bards of Wales had a very high standing; they were singers and poets, and they played the telyn (the Welsh harp) and crwth, which was a solo as well as an accompanying instrument. This early crwth is thought to have developed from the much older lyre, a plucked string instrument associated with the god Apollo; there are other European "bowed lyre" folk instruments. Ancient manuscripts giving rules for the crwth show that its playing was complex and difficult. The lower

Medieval crwth

Medieval guitar-fiddle

uncrowned bards were allowed a three-stringed crwth only, and had to play standing, a sign of inferiority; they were sometimes called "weeds" and considered to further the work of the devil, presumably because they played for revels and dancing among the people.

Many different forms of bowed instruments were played in medieval Europe; they came here slowly and in small numbers, and did not at first take the place of the English harp. In the kingdoms of Southern Europe, minstrels played the guitar fiddle in various forms, and the oval fiddle from Spain. In France, the fiddle was called the viele, and fiddlers were held in high esteem for their playing for song and dance; present-day folk fiddlers are thus carrying on a very old tradition. Northern minstrels played the less-waisted Minnesinger fiddle; the Minnesingers were the troubadours and minstrels of the North, and the Minnesinger fiddle is often seen in English pictures and carvings of the time. The lyra is a

The Minnesinger fiddle   *Eleventh-century lyra*

very old stringed instrument—one is shown in an eleventh-century Anglo Saxon manuscript; it is often confused with the rebec, being similar in shape and often having three strings. The latter, however, came later to Europe from the Near East where it was called the rebab; it was further developed in Europe, and a larger form was known as the rybybe, the finger-board is markedly raised above the sound-box (see p. 35), and the strings are stopped by pressing them down on to this finger-board—as in the violin. The lyra has no finger-board, and the strings are stopped by pushing against them with the flat of the finger-nail; some European folk instruments are played like this today, and the hurdy-gurdy (see p. 100) works on this principle. The sound is different, more buzzing, and the notes slide into one another, as in *glissando* violin-playing or Hawaiian guitar.

Some of the early bowed instruments had only one or two stopped or melody strings, with pairs of bourdon strings on either side; this arrangement is also seen in the hurdy-gurdy; similar instruments are portrayed being plucked instead of bowed. Experts agree that there is no evi-

Thirteenth-century rybybe

Tenth-century Spanish oval fiddle. Only the middle string is stopped

dence of bowed stringed instruments in Europe earlier than the tenth century. However, one sometimes finds them mentioned in translations from earlier writings; this may be due to inaccurate translation, or to the fact that over the years the name for one instrument became applied to others. Thus in the great days of the Irish kingdoms, before the sack by the Northmen in the ninth century, the crot or cruit was a kind of harp; later the same word became the crwth or crowd, which in its turn could cover the fiddle as well. The translators of the Bible, faced with lists of instruments which at that time were strange and unknown, gave them names of instruments familiar to their readers. This has caused much confusion; however, research has now provided us with more accurate names and pictures for these instruments.

The student who looks at the medieval carvings, stained glass, and illustrated manuscripts of Europe will see a great variety of stringed instruments, bearing witness to the change and experiment that went on among those instruments from which, in time, such things as the familiar violin or guitar were to emerge. In remote and mountainous parts of Europe, instruments are played that appear to have changed little from medieval times, and it is to these that he must listen if he wants an idea as to how the ancient instruments were played, and sounded, which is, after all, the most important thing about any musical instrument. Fortunately for us, we are able to do this, since recordings have been made by folklorists and musicians, while other groups of musicians have made replicas of medieval instruments on which they play the music of that time.

A common childhood accomplishment of the inter-war years

6   THE PIANOFORTE

NO ONE CAN GO FAR without hearing a piano. There are pianos in schools, pubs and clubs; one piano can be played in turn for a youth club, a Darby and Joan, a jazz group, country dancing and hymn practice. There are pianos in many homes, but they are not played as often as in the years before the war when most children learned the piano as a matter of course. Many of these pianos were bought during the short time of prosperity during the First World War, when working people were able to afford them; boys and men usually had the chance to play in a brass or silver band, but until the family could afford a piano there was not much for the girls to play.

In those days the "wireless" was a new invention, and the gramophone difficult to amplify. So the piano was played for singing and dancing, and was part of every dance band, whether professional or one of the amateur bands that played for local hops. It was also the chief accompaniment to the silent pictures, a piano score coming with the reels of film. There were travelling concert parties and Pierrot troupes, and the accompanist, who was at the piano all the time, was indispensable.

Much of this music was influenced by jazz. Jazz and Ragtime were born in the years following the American Civil War when the liberated Negroes, wandering in search of work, picked up any instrument they could and played it in their own way. In saloons and dives they found battered old pianos; that these were out of tune did not matter, since "flatting" of some notes suited the harmony of the blues; they used them rather as their ancestors had used the speaking drums, playing intertwining rhythms and melodies at the same time.

In Victorian times, the piano could be heard at concerts and in musichalls and pubs, but fewer people could afford one at home. Those who

Mid-nineteenth-century grand piano

*The Victorian piano as
an instrument of torture*

could, often wanted to show off their wealth, and the piano was elabor-
ately decorated, and sometimes too covered up with runners, orna-
ments, and photo-frames, for serious music. Nevertheless, piano solos
were part of a social evening, and much showy music was composed, full
of "runabouts and twiddles". Piano playing was considered an essential
accomplishment of young ladies; a working man in Mrs. Gaskell's book
Mary Barton speaks with contempt of "a do-nothing lady, worrying
shopmen all morning, and screeching at her pianny all afternoon". The
editor of a book about women's work, however, sympathized with the
young ladies "shut up in the schoolroom with a French Grammar and a
Piano as instruments of torture". For many girls the long hours of dull
practice were indeed torture, but for others music was an escape from
their tedious and narrow lives.

Early upright by Stodart, London, 1801. The hammer mechanism is behind the lower part of the soundboard, and could be seen by opening the back of the instrument. The hammer heads can be seen below the girl's hand

One reason for the popularity of the piano was the construction of the upright piano, sometimes called the Cottage Piano, the Piccolo Piano, or the Pianino, which took up much less room than the grand; makers experimented with this early in the nineteenth century. The first iron frame piano was made in 1800 in America where makers were experimenting with iron frames; this was a very important development for several reasons, the most important being that of "pull". The sound of the notes depends on the length and weight of the wire strings, and on their tension; this tension is called "pull" and is measured in terms of weight; a modern grand may have a total pull of as much as thirty tons. Iron frames could stand a far greater pull than the old wooden ones, and thicker and longer strings could be used, giving a much louder and more resonant sound. By 1860 the American makers had perfected the iron-frame piano, and mass-produced them in factories. Makers elsewhere did the same, and there were soon plenty of cheaper factory-made pianos for all who could afford them.

Before this, pianos were made in workshops by craftsmen, and were scarce and dear; in fact, many people never even heard one. Great skill was needed, and the materials carefully prepared; unseasoned wood, for instance, could warp or shrink, and this would send the instrument out of tune. The wood of which the box of keyboard instruments is made is very important; it must be light, and responsive to the vibrations of the strings and the air inside it; if it becomes clogged up with damp, the sound is dull and poor. Both square and grand pianos did go out of tune easily, and a tuner attended concerts in order to tune up the instrument during the interval. The sound, although soft, was clear and sweet. The upper classes and newly rich had the square pianos, so popular for the parlours; young ladies, like Jane Austen's heroines, were expected to delight the company with singing and playing, and also to play when the company at home wanted to dance.

The first square pianos were made in the seventeen sixties; some of the earliest were oblong boxes which could be put on a table like the smaller clavichords and spinets that were popular at the time, the strings running longways across the box. They were introduced into England by

47

"Square" piano, early nineteenth century

A Zumpe table piano; behind, a clavichord

Johannes Zumpe, a German refugee from the Seven Years War, who had been a pupil of Silbermann, the earliest German maker of pianofortes. Dr. Charles Burney wrote about the new pianos with enthusiasm: "These, from their low price and the convenience of their form, as well as the power of expression, suddenly grew into such favour that there was scarcely a house in the kingdom where a keyed instrument had ever had admission, but was supplied with one of Zumpe's pianofortes."

There were other refugee craftsmen, twelve in particular who were called the Twelve Apostles. The daughter of Tschudi, one of these men, married one of his young workmen, John Broadwood, who became his partner and successor, and founded the firm of Broadwood and Sons; at this time British pianofortes were the best in Europe.

The other popular keyboard instruments were the harpsichord, the spinet, and the clavichord. The harpsichord is shaped somewhat like a lying-down harp, and the spinet is a smaller wing-shaped instrument; in both, the strings are plucked from below by quills or plectra attached to jacks operated from the keyboard. They thus work on a different principle from the piano, and have a crisp plucked-string quality, more

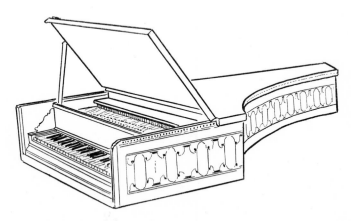

Italian harpsichord of 1521. The jacks are under the bridge below the hinge of the lid

D

Sixteenth-century spinet

clear and precise than that of the harp and other instruments where the fingers are in actual contact with the string. Much of the consort and early orchestral music was conducted from the harpsichord, the player supplying harmonies and time; this music called for precision, and the harpsichord provided this. Mechanical devices, operated by pedals or stops, brought extra strings and jacks into play for varying tone qualities and volume.

The spinet was played only in the home, a delicate-sounding instrument suitable to accompany a solo voice, or for keyboard music; Pepys had a "little triangle", presumably a form of spinet. (The later box pianos are sometimes wrongly called spinets). The earlier form of both

Sixteenth-century virginals

spinet and harpsichord was the virginals, a boxlike instrument with strings plucked by quills; it was popular during the sixteenth century, and found alike in barbers' shops and the Queen's apartments.

The Clavichord is an expressive instrument, capable of *crescendo* and *diminuendo* by touch, but its tone is very soft, and in those days the strings quickly went out of tune. The strings were touched from below by small metal tangents operated from the keyboard; it dates from the fifteenth century.

It was natural that at a time when the character of music was changing —it was the time of Bach and Handel—the instrument makers of Europe would try to make an instrument that was expressive and at the same time powerful. A man had been touring Europe with a very large dulcimer which was played by striking the strings with hammers with great dexterity, and experiments were made with the idea of hammers operated from a keyboard. This was far from simple: the hammer must fall back as soon as it has struck the string (this is known as the escapement mechanism) or else it will deaden the sound by preventing the vibration of the string. But if the vibrations of each string struck were allowed to die out naturally, the sounds would get mixed up as they do when the piano is played with the loud pedal on all the time. Therefore there had to be a damper mechanism to stop the vibrations as soon as the player's finger left the key; the soft pedal checks the vibrations even more.

The first instrument maker to combine these mechanisms was Cristofori of Florence; as early as 1709, he made what he called a Gravecembalo col piano e forte: a "harpsichord with soft and loud"—although it was a harpsichord only in shape. His early instruments were not popular, as they were far from perfect. There is so much to be considered in a pianoforte: the mechanism must work smoothly for rapid playing; it must be sensitive to slight differences in touch; it must stay in tune; the louder lower notes must not swamp the weaker high notes (a modern piano has three strings to each high note, two for the middle range, and one only for each low note). Over the centuries the instrument has been altered and improved by generations of pianoforte makers, first in Europe, and later in America as well. What was once a curiosity has now become part of everyday life, and anyone who loves music and is not afraid of practising can play, in their own home, music composed especially for the piano, or can extemporize as the first jazz men did. Cristofori's name remains, the "soft and loud", the Piano e Forte.

Playing the virginals. Note the way of holding the hands; the little finger was not used

Cristofori's pianoforte

Drawing-room music in the early nineteenth century

7

THE "ENGLISH HARP", the national instrument of medieval times, has been developed by makers and musicians in various countries, and is now rarely played outside the orchestra. The "fair performers" seated at this instrument, romantic alike in sound and appearance, were early Victorian and before them, Regency and eighteenth-century ladies, sweeping the strings with picturesque gestures while their escorts trilled away on the flute. After 1810 they would play the double action and before then the single-action pedal harps. Briefly, the pedals enable strings to be raised by half tones, so that the player can use sharps and flats other than those of the diatonic in which the harp is tuned.

These harps were so large, and difficult to play, that makers of the early nineteenth century produced a number of small and elegant

Harp-lute, early nineteenth century

drawing-room instruments advertised as giving the authentic harp sound while being "incredibly easy" to master. These, of which the harp-lute is one, had fretted finger-boards and guitar tuning as well as free strings.

But if the concert harp has changed a great deal, the Celtic harp or Clarsach has changed very little. It is now played for Irish and Gaelic folksong in the same form as it was played by the famous Irish harpers of the eighteenth century. It has from thirty to fifty brass strings tuned to a diatonic scale; these can be tightened for accidentals by tuning keys or hooks. It is now played with the fingers, but the old harpers grew their nails long and struck the strings between nail and finger-tip, giving greater resonance; at the same time, another finger was ready to dampen the string when needed so that each note could sound clear and distinct. This way was last observed in 1792, at a gathering of old harpers, being used by the oldest of all, blind Dennis O'Hempsey. Although there were

The clarsach or Celtic harp,
showing the tuning key

The Welsh triple harp

revivals after this gathering, these harpers were the last of the line of bardic harpers that stretched back to the earliest records of the Irish kingdoms where their ancestors had been second in rank only to the kings.
Irish harpers not only played the old tunes, but many of them, like
O'Carolan who lived through the tumultuous years when William of
Orange was attempting to "settle" Ireland, were also composers. Eighteenth-century Irish gentlemen still kept their own harpers and pipers, but
their status as bards had dwindled with the gradual break-up of the old
kingdoms under William III, Cromwell, Elizabeth I and the earlier con-
quests of Ireland. Ordinary people, too, played, and a historian of 1636
noted that few Irish men or women could not play the harp.

During the last century, most Welsh harpers adopted the concert
harp, and there are very few now who can play the triple harp. The
Chapel movement of the eighteenth and nineteenth centuries discour-
aged the playing of harp and crwth in favour of hymn singing, and so the
harpers who were once found in every village and hamlet are now few.
(On the other hand, the choirs are many, and the hymnal abounds with
Welsh folk airs). The triple harp originated in Italy, and was adapted
and played with great skill by the harpers of Wales; it has three rows of
strings, the outer two tuned to the diatonic and the inner row provid-
ing the accidentals, and it is very difficult to play. As early as the sixteenth century they had made the first chromatic harp, with two rows of
strings. Like the Irish, their harpers came of a long line going back to the
bards of the old kingdoms, and the telyn or Welsh harp developed from
the clarsach and the earlier forms of harp played by the Celtic peoples
of Ireland, Wales and Scotland.

In Scotland, where the highland pipes took the place of the harp as a
national instrument, Irish harpers had often been employed by Scottish
nobles, and the clarsach adopted by Scots players. James VI of Scotland
and I of England played it, and it then enjoyed a wave of popularity in
England.

Elizabeth I had an Irish harper, and Francis Bacon wrote "No harp
hath the sound so melting and prolonged as the Irish harp". In Ireland
the harpers were so reverenced "that in the time of rebellion they (the

Irish) will forbear to hurt neither their persons or their goods"; but the harpers were persecuted by English and Viking invaders because, like the pipers, they had so great an influence over the people through their high standing and the power of their music that they were dangerous to occupying powers. The medieval clarsach was smaller than its successors, and there were different versions, some with a much steeper upward curve to the end of the neck, more like that of the telyn. However, the essential shape of both modern clarsach and the fourteenth-century Trinity College harp in Dublin is much the same.

Medieval telyn and clarsach

Welsh harpers were also famous and widely travelled. Under the medieval laws of Wales three things were necessary to a man in his home: a virtuous wife, a cushion on his chair, and a well-tuned harp; not only the bards, but all true Welshmen played the harp. It was so important to a man that it was the only thing that could not be seized for debt; without it, he was no better than a slave. During the fourteenth century, the Irish brought the gut-strung clarsach to Wales. Hitherto, the Welsh had strung their harps with horsehair, and the Irish called them "buzzers".

The bard Davydde ab Gwylim wrote in the fourteenth century contrasting the clarsach and its gut strings, its curved pillar and swelling sound-board, with the telyn, horse hair strung, and with a straight pillar and flat sound-box; the sound of the clarsach, he complained, was like "a lame goose amongst the corn, a squealing foolish Irish witch". However, the Welsh adopted the gut strings, and later the metal strings which the Irish were the first to use. In 1186, Geraldus Cambrensis, the Norman Archbishop of Wales, visited Ireland, and his comparison of the harp-playing of Wales and Ireland allowed that the former was "of a grave and solemn nature, whereas that of the Irish was soft, lively, and melodious, their fingers moving rapidly over the strings".

The harp was the national instrument of medieval England, the Cythara Anglica being in shape much like a clarsach (see p. 9). Kings and nobles had their own harpers, Norman nobles employing Irish players. Before this, it was held in high esteem by the Saxons who called it the joy-wood and considered its playing to be an essential accomplishment for a nobleman. The Utrecht Psalter, shows an older and simpler form, more like those of Eastern Europe and Asia. Little is known about the earlier harps played alike by the Celtic bards and Nordic scalds, who sang of gods and heroes, and were held in great reverence; in early days the scalds were believed to have descended from the gods.

Angle-harp from the Utrecht psalter, ninth century and possibly older

Tin whistle played for Britannia Coconut Dance

8   WHISTLE PIPES AND RECORDERS

PUT VERY BRIEFLY, the principle of flutes is this: a column of air in an open-ended tube is set in vibration by a stream of air blown against the edge of a hole in the side. For the transverse flute, this wind-stream comes directly from the mouth; for the fipple flute, or flute-à-bec, it is channelled through a mouthpiece. The pitch of the note depends on the length of the air-column; finger holes in the tube, to be uncovered at will shorten this and produce higher notes; still higher notes can be obtained by overblowing to sound harmonics. The longer the tube, the greater the range of notes that can be played; pitch and tone depend too, on the bore (inside shape) of the tube, a wide bore making a louder note, and a conical bore a different tone.

The six-holed tin whistle—the penny whistle of our Victorian ancestors—is the simplest sort of fipple flute. All finger-holes covered, it plays the Tonic—that is, the Keynote or Doh; by overblowing, the player gets the first harmonic, the Tonic an octave higher; thus he can play two octaves, and by half covering the appropriate hole, he obtains semitones. This instrument is still to be bought under the misnomer of the "English flageolet". Years ago it was much more common, and most children bought one at some time or other. Henry Mayhew, in his studies for *London Labour and the London Poor*, interviewed a "Whistling and Dancing Boy" whose trade was to dance to his own tin whistle, on the street and in pubs or private houses; one of the boy's accomplishments was to put the mouthpiece up one nostril, and play that way.

Modern descant and treble recorders

The tin whistle is played with incredible speed and effect by folk players, and is the traditional music for the Britannia Coconut dance of Bacup when the dancers black their faces and dance through the streets with wooden discs at their knees and belts, and clap them with discs in their hands. It was played a good deal during the early Industrial Revolution, players having ready access to metal tubing. It is possible to make a whistle of this kind from a hollow stick, as our ancestors must often have done; indeed, many children make and play similar bamboo pipes while still at junior school; these pipes are larger than the tin whistle, and their sound more deep and full.

Schools also have recorder groups (the old term is a Consort of recorders). The recorder, in its heyday known as the English flute, is a fipple flute with eight holes, one being a "speaker hole" at the back;

Recorder consort, c. 1700. Bass, two treble, descant, tenor

by partially or completely opening this hole, and by a system of cross-fingering, as well as by some overblowing, it is possible to get a two octave chromatic scale. As the writer of the sixteenth-century Leckingfelde Proverbs wrote: "Manyfolde fyngerynge and stoppes bryngithe from him his tunes clere." The contracting bore gives it a more mellow tone than the whistle and transverse flute. Although popular since its revival here, it had previously fallen into disuse; while the recorder consort suited the counterpoint and musical pattern of Renaissance music, later music called for more volume and expression, which were provided by other instruments then being developed.

Seventeenth-century recorders were made in three sections, but the earlier ones were in one piece, and had a wider bore and were louder. Some were double: the pitches of the two pipes, by differing very slightly, vibrate together in such a way as to give more volume. During these centuries much music was composed for the recorder consort, and the groups could also play music scored for several voices. A set of recorders, suitable for family playing, was kept in a panpipe-shaped case,

Late medieval double recorder

Seventeenth-century contrebass recorder
(after Mersenne)

and usually included two descants, trebles, and tenors, and a bass; the Great Consort included not only smaller descants for very high parts, but Quart and Quint Bass, and the Great Bass, or Contra Bass. Henry VIII had 154 flutes and recorders: 27 of ivory, 2 of glass, and some with silver-gilt or gold tips, and all in cases lined with velvet.

Before this, it was a minstrel instrument which was developed some time during the fourteenth century; like the tabor pipe, it was played with a drum for dancing, and its sound was loud and shrill. The name comes from the old meaning of "record": to sing like a bird; anyone who has heard a facsimile of one of these old recorders can have no doubt that it was well named.

The flageolet is the little cousin of the recorder. Originally it had six holes, two at the back; during the last century, it shared in improvements in range and tone made to all woodwind instruments, and had five or more keys, and there were double and triple flageolets. The French "Quadrille" single flageolet was popular in dance bands during the mid-nineteenth-century fashion for the dance called quadrille; according to a catalogue of 1870, it was not only easier to learn than the flute, but was more "powerful and showy". (It was a time for showy music.)

The flageolet had no place in eighteenth-century orchestral music, but was found among the people whenever an air or a jig was called for during work breaks or leisure hours—such as they were. In the seventeenth century it was also a musical toy for gentlemen; Pepys wrote of "my new little flageolet that is so soft; it pleases me mightily". A tutor for it, *The Pleasant Companion*, was published in 1661, in which the author, Thomas Greeting, Gent., says that the flageolet is "fitly termed a Pleasant Companion, for it may be carried in the pocket, and bear one

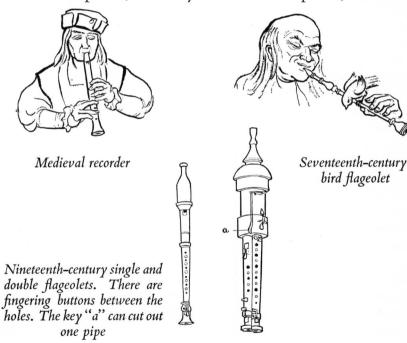

Medieval recorder

Seventeenth-century bird flageolet

Nineteenth-century single and double flageolets. There are fingering buttons between the holes. The key "a" can cut out one pipe

Company either by Land or Water". This was a time when people enjoyed music and other parties on the Thames.

There was also a slender little high-pitched Bird Flageolet, used to imitate birdsong and, apparently, to teach cage birds new songs; a little book, *The Bird Fancyer's Delight*, was published in 1697, giving instruction "Concerning the Teaching of all sorts of Singing Birds after the Flageolet and Flute when rightly made".

The flageolet was first made in France in 1581; its ancestor was the shepherd's pipe, common ancestor of all whistle pipes. Another pipe was the tabor pipe, which has three holes, and is played by the left hand only, while the right hand beats a small snared drum or tabor slung on the left arm; by cross-fingering and overblowing the player can sound at least eleven notes. Known locally as Whittle and Dub, and the tabor decorated with red, yellow and green morris ribbons, they provide the traditional music for morris dancing (see p. 8), and, until about a hundred years ago, could be heard in every village in Oxfordshire and elsewhere in England, playing for the Whitsun dances as they had done for the previous 600 years. In the fifteenth century and before, pipe and tabor were minstrels' instruments, and can be seen in the carved minstrels' galleries put up in some churches and cathedrals by the order of the minstrels' Guilds; the players were, however, among the lower class of minstrels, and had to play standing and for only a penny a day.

Pipe and tabor were a frequent accompaniment to travelling entertainers (see p. 92): dancers, tumblers, acrobats, performing animals, men disguised in animals' skins, and all the company in rags, jags, and velvet gown who came to town on fair days and holy days, and put on their shows in villages and castle yards on their way. The beat of tabor and shrilling of the pipe heralded entertainment, however unrespectable, and would certainly have brought our ancestors out to see what was going on.

Pipe and tabor came here from the great centre of early medieval culture and minstrelsy, the kingdoms of Southern France and Northern Spain, where they can still sometimes be heard, playing for traditional and ancient dances.

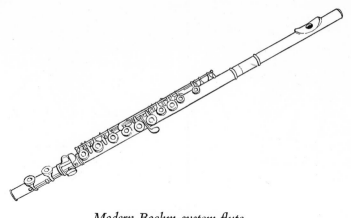

Modern Boehm-system flute

9

NOWADAYS, THE FLUTE is chiefly associated with the orchestra, as is the fife with military and other bands. The sixteenth-century bass flute is now coming back into favour; the half-size flute, the piccolo, as well as being in the orchestra, has always been a favourite among those who like a handy little instrument to play for their own and other's entertainment. Both flute and piccolo were drawing-room instruments in Dickens's days, the flute being the more aristocratic and poetic. In the first quarter of the nineteenth century it was immensely popular; there were many experiments with different keys and fingering, and professors of the flute abounded, each claiming his own system to be the best. It was into this "hive of flute-blowing busybodies", as Adam Carse describes it, that Theobald Boehm came in 1831. Boehm, trained as a jeweller, was a flautist and also a scientist interested in the construction of musical instruments. He reconstructed the flute, and applied a system of mechanism and fingering which is now in general use, and has been applied to some other wood-wind instruments.

Flute-blowing busybodies

The modern flute has a varying number of keys; the boxwood flute for which Beethoven composed had six to eight, and Mozart's had but one. This was a gentleman's instrument in the eighteenth century, since harpsichord, harp and piano were considered too effeminate, and the violin too suggestive of the common fiddle. It was known as the German flute, as it was there that it was first incorporated into the orchestra in preference to the English or common flute (the recorder). The direct breath control and use of the tongue and lips made it a very expressive instrument with effective techniques of *vibrato* and trilling.

Possibly because of this expressiveness, it has been associated with love. In common with some other eighteenth-century instruments, it was sometimes pitched a minor third below the normal key, and called the

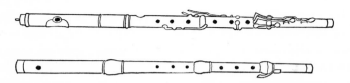

(a) Nicholson's improved flute, 1820, made by Prowse, (b) Stanesby one-key flute, c. 1750

flute d'amour or flute d'amore; as such, its soulful music was much admired. The association with courtship and fertility rites is far older and more widespread, and this may have accounted for the opposition it met with at various times from puritanical elders; the six-holed flute of the seventeenth century moved Stephen Gosson, a Puritan pamphleteer, to condemn fluteplayers among the "caterpillars of the Commonwealth". John Bunyan, however, when imprisoned for his Puritan faith, made himself a flute from a chair leg to cheer his lonely years behind bars.

There were flute consorts in the sixteenth century, and it was played alone or with other instruments to accompany singing. It was played all over Europe in medieval times, especially in Germany, where it was an instrument favoured by the most aristocratic of the Minnesingers. It was also a peasants' instrument, fashioned, like the whistles and the reed pipes, from hollow bones and reeds by shepherds and herdsmen while guarding their beasts on the hills and mountains.

Eighteenth-century one-key flute played as accompaniment to singing

Medieval flute

Panpipe band, c. 1800

10

THE PANPIPES, or syrinx, is one of the oldest of instruments; it was known to the Ancient Greeks, and to earlier civilizations. It survives in Europe as a folk instrument, but is found here only as a plastic toy. Panpipes are a series of end-blown flutes—that is, cylinders, across the top end of which the player blows—graduated in size to make a scale, and bound together,or cut from one piece of wood.

There were, in the early nineteenth century, panpipe bands playing in Vauxhall Gardens; the players, exotically dressed, stuck the pipes in the front of their jackets, and played percussion instruments with their hands.

Panpipes are the traditional accompanying music for Punch and Judy, and probably came here from Italy with Puncinello himself. They are no longer heard, but were well known as such in Dickens's time; readers will remember Little Nell's adventures with the Punch and Judy men, one of whom, to attract an audience, "flourished hysterically on the pipes, and played an air"; the air was traditional, and very old. Called Pandean pipes, they were adopted by other travelling musicians and entertainers of those times.

One or two early manuscripts show minstrels playing similar pipes bound so as to make a circular instrument, and the simple syrinx was played by shepherds and peasant players here as in Europe.

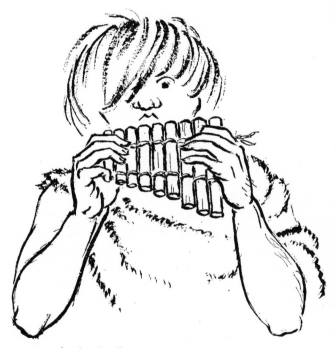

Simple shepherd's syrinx made from separate pipes

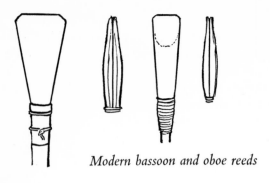

Modern bassoon and oboe reeds

11 REED PIPES

THE AIR COLUMN in the tube of reed instruments is set in vibration by either a single or double reed. The single reed is a thin tongue cut from the side of a reed tube or bound on to the mouthpiece so that it beats against an aperture when the player blows. The double reed has two fanning out tongues of cane which beat against each other. Oboe and bassoon and other past and present members of their family have double-reed mouthpieces, and the clarinet and saxophone single reeds. They are mainly played in orchestras and bands, but the clarinet, like the flute, was in Victorian times a drawing-room instrument for gentlemen; as it was also a military instrument, it was considered a manly thing to play.

In the early part of this century, before the cinema or "the wireless" was part of everyday life, there were, as well as professional concert parties and Pierrot troupes, many groups of people who got together to entertain themselves and their friends and relations. They also put on shows to help good causes, and to amuse those in Homes and institutions. There were songs, sentimental and comic, recitations, sketches, and instrumental items; the clarinet was often heard, and even if it whistled and squawked in unskilled hands, it was well received.

Modern clarinet, and mouthpiece with single reed in place

Both clarinet and saxophone have become jazz instruments, and the latter played a large part in the big dance bands of the inter-war years, which provided the pop of that time, and showed jazz influence, especially in instrumentation. Dance band saxes were played in a moaning fashion; the clarinets shared this technique, lacking the clarity of either concert or jazz clarinet. Both instruments came early into the jazz scene, because they were among the ex-military band instruments found second-hand in New Orleans and other cities. Most military clarinets are the smaller high-pitched models, and in jazz they played the role of female voice to the male of the trombone.

The sax was invented in 1846 by Adolphe Sax, to be a supporting instrument to the clarinets in the band; it has a clarinet mouthpiece and fingering, but a wide conical brass tube giving a powerful tone suitable

Tenor saxophone, 1840

(a) Three-keyed oboe.
(b) Five-keyed clarinet.
Both c. 1800

for outdoor music. Like the clarinet, its sizes range between the small soprano and the large bass model, the alto and tenor being most used in
orchestras and bands.

The clarinet has the widest range of any of the woodwind, and great
variation of tone and expression; the present clarinet has thirteen keys. It
has undergone many changes; it was the five-keyed boxwood clarinet of
which Mozart realized the possibilities, although it was extremely tricky
to play. This clarinet, and some later models, were played in the village
Church bands during the eighteenth and nineteenth centuries, as were

flutes, oboes, and sometimes the old four-keyed bassoons. This group of instruments, too, made up the wind bands which were to be found in many of the villages where there were cottage industries, and weavers, spinners, or metal workers got together for music. (It was from such villages that the great brass band movement was to come in later years.)

The first eight-holed two-keyed clarinets were constructed in the late seventeenth century by Johann Denner, instrument maker of Nuremburg, a city famous for the foundries where brass instruments were made. In the sixteen-fifties a bagpipe maker from Normandy famous for his improvements to the flute, Jacques Hotteterre, and his associates constructed the oboe family and the bassoons. Constructed, not invented; in each case there were older reed instruments of the same sort. Denner and Hotteterre improved on these, and thus created the instruments that are part of the modern musical scene.

Single and double-reed pipes were played all over Europe, as they had been for generations. The double reed shawm and pommer were

Village wind band, with bassoon, five-keyed clarinet, one-keyed flute and two-keyed oboe

Denner's two-keyed clarinet and his one-keyed chalumeau (drawn to scale). The chalumeau was originally a shepherd's pipe

The curtal

processional instruments, their loud tones suitable for outdoor music; the crumhorns were made in different keys for consort music; the curtals, forerunners of the bassoon, provided bass parts. In France there were consorts of the single-reed chalumeau, a shepherd's pipe still played in Southern France for folk dancing.

As late as the eighteenth century, the hornpipe was still played in Scotland, where it was called the stockhorn, and in Wales, where it was called the pibcorn (pipehorn). Of unknown antiquity, it has a six-holed pipe of wood or bone, the reed at one end and a cow-horn bell at the other. The tongue was cut out of the side of the reed, not made separately, and carefully pared down, especially at the point of attachment, so that it could vibrate easily; over this there was a horn mouthpiece to act as wind chest. Like other folk instruments, the hornpipe was used for song and dance; in Wales it was probably a bardic instrument in the great days of the Welsh kingdoms. A pipehorn is referred to in an eighth-century manuscript; similar pipes were doubtless played long before that.

Reed pipes were sometimes played in pairs, so that the melody could be doubled, or were supported by a drone. This was important to medieval and folk music as there was often only one instrument available; therefore they needed to make as much noise as possible.

Reed pipes were shepherds' instruments, as they could be made from reeds growing by the water, or from straw and green corn. Before cheap harmonicas and tin whistles could be bought, boys used to make themselves "squeakers" which were straw pipes much the same as those Mersenne illustrated in his *Harmonie Universelle* in 1637. (Father Pierre Mersenne, philosopher, mathematician and musician, wrote in detail about the music and instruments of his time.) Milton wrote of "scrannel pipes of wretched straw" and Shakespeare of shepherds who "pipe on oaten straws" and long before that Chaucer ended a list of wind instruments with

> "Pypes made of greene corne
> As han these litel herdegromes
> That kepen bestes in the bromes."

As old, and still heard in recent times, was the Whit-horn, traditionally played at Whitsun, made of coiled bark held together with thorns, and with a single-reed mouthpiece stuck in the narrow end.

Reed pipes have a long history in ancient Greece, and before that; as far as this country is concerned they can be left with the litel herdegromes that have kepen their bestes on the common land ever since pastoral people have lived here.

The pibcorn, with single reed

Mersenne's reed pipe, and shepherd boy player

Northumbrian small-pipes

"... IN THE XXIX DAY of Decembre, to a drone bagpiper that plaed and song before the lades, VIId." This item of royal expenditure dates from the reign of Henry VIII, when bagpipes were played all over the British Isles, by royal minstrel and shepherd alike. They were also played, as today, in most of Europe and large areas in the Near East, Asia and India. There are at least nine types of bagpipe now played in Europe alone. In this country we can hear, in addition to the Irish and Scottish war pipes, the Irish Uillean pipes and the Northumbrian smallpipes.

The sound of the small-pipes is sweet and delicate, and their range of notes and expression is wide. The chanter (the melody pipe) has a very thin double reed, and nine or more keys; the end is stopped so that if the player closes all the stops and finger-holes at once he makes no sound at all. In this way he can use rests and pauses, and play *staccato* as well as *legato*. The four single-reed drones, of which three are played at a time, are set in one stock, and can be tuned to different notes. (The stocks are wooden cylinders, fixed into the bag, into which the pipes are inserted; early pipers invented this so that the pipes could easily be taken out for repairs to the reeds and replaced.) With his right elbow the player works the bellows, and with the left arm he controls the air pressure from the bag into the pipes. Small-pipe players often made their own pipes, and composed some of their music, as did the Northumbrian miner Tom Clough who died recently and was called a "Prince of Pipers".

The Northumbrian Guild of Pipers keep alive these inherited skills. In previous centuries, however, the small-pipes were often heard in the North of England, playing for singing and dancing and all occasions when the people gathered together. It is thought they were developed from the French musette, a small bellows-blown bagpipe popular in the French court of the seventeenth century, and itself adapted from the shepherds' bagpipes.

The Union or Uillean (elbow) pipes (see frontispiece) have the widest range of notes of any pipes, and are louder than the small-pipes. The double reed chanter has four keys, and the open end can be stopped against the pipers' apron strapped above the player's right knee, so it is possible for him to make a break in the sound. It has three single-reed drones, and three or four double-reed regulator pipes with keys controlled by the wrist and lower side of the right hand. The regulators provide a chordal accompaniment, and can bring in an effective blaze of sound. They were added to the pipes during the last century, when there were many pipers in Ireland, both folk players, and "gentleman players" who gave concerts; not for the first time, the fame of Irish pipers spread beyond their native land. In the eighteenth century, and before, gentlemen had their own pipers as well as harpers, and among the people the pipes were heard at all gatherings from fairs to weddings. Pipers, like the harpers, were persecuted by invading forces because their music could rally and inspire the people; moreover, travelling as they did, they could carry secret messages. The elbow pipes date from around 1600; before that the Irish played the Piob Mor, war pipes with two drones and a mouth pipe to fill the bag.

Another bellows-blown instrument was the Lowland bagpipe, now heard no more. These had the same scale and chanter as the Highland but were softer and suited to folk music rather than battle. The bagpipes had two tenor and one bass drone set in one stock, and a conical double-reed chanter with no keys. As with all the older pipes, the windflow, regulated by the pressure of the arm and wrist, was continuous, and as the chanters had open ends the sound could not stop until the bag was empty. The Highland pipe player is faced with this same situation, and since he cannot articulate the notes by tonguing as can the player of any non-bagpipe, nor can differentiate between them by closing all the holes as a small-pipe player can, he has to make the notes clear by skilful

78

Lowland pipes

fingering techniques. The most common of these is "gracing", that is flicking a grace note, often a lower one, in between the notes of a melody. The Lowland pipes were often played for dancing, and a skilled player could play, sing and dance all at the same time.

The only pipes now played in Scotland are the Great Highland pipes; they are mouth-filled, with a long blow pipe that enables the player to keep his head up in correct military style, and their great volume is well suited to outdoor and processional music. The chanters are conical with expanding bore, giving a different tone from the cylindrical chanters of the small-pipes; they have three drones in separate stocks, one being the Great Drone, a bass drone, which was added round about 1700, after which time the pipes became almost exclusively military instruments, and

Great Highland pipes, with drone   *Highland pipes, c. 1740*
and chanter reeds

drum and pipe bands were incorporated into Highland regiments. Now, however, since neither the old Highland nor the Lowland pipes are played, they have had to take over some of their functions, notably the Highland dances.

The two-drone Highland pipes were however also war pipes, and accompanied Highlanders into battle. After the defeat of Culloden clansmen and pipers were scattered, and the piping skills and the pibrochs were almost silenced. The pibrochs are series of tunes and variations, each group suitable for a special occasion, such as going into battle or mourning the dead. In Ireland, where for many centuries folk pipes and war pipes flourished together, the war pipes played for funeral processions.

The Highland pipes were also played for dancing and festive occasions, and Scottish lairds had their own pipers; there were town pipers, paid to pipe through the streets at certain hours, and folk pipers, some of whom got into trouble for playing on the Sabbath. An English traveller, Thomas Kirke, wrote in 1679 of Scotsmen admiring "loud terrene noises, like the bellowing of beasts; the loud bagpipe is their delight". There were also schools of piping, the most famous being in Skye, where Donald MacCrimmon, a distinguished Irish piper, became, around 1600, piper to the MacLeods; his descendants continued in that office until the death of the last of the line in 1845, and pipers came from afar to learn from the

Chaucer's Miller on pilgrimage with his bagpipes

MacCrimmons. The Piob Mor are thought to have come from Ireland in the sixteenth century; however, bagpipes were played in Scotland before then, as they were in Europe and the rest of the British Isles; they were the smaller pipes, with one or two drones, and less volume than the war pipes.

Such bagpipes were played in Lincolnshire, which was famous for its pipers, as late as the nineteenth century, but during that and the preceding century they had died out in England. In the seventeenth century, when Milton wrote of bagpipe and rebec playing for rustic revelry, they were common folk instruments. In 1603 Robert Armin in *Nest of Ninnies* put the situation clearly when describing Christmas cheer in the house of a knight: "A noise of minstrels and a Lincolnshire bagpipe was prepared; the minstrels for the great chamber, the bagpipe for the hall; the minstrels to serve up the knight's meat and the bagpipe for the common dancing". Playing during the serving of meals to the nobility was common; Queen Elizabeth's band, which in 1587 included a bagpipe, would often have performed that office. Both Henry VIII and his father had a bagpiper in their bands, the former owning "a bagge pipe with pipes of ivorie, the bagge covered with purple vellat".

However, the bagpipe was for the most part a folk instrument, connected with dancing, especially the May dances. It was also played by pilgrims on the long roads to holy places; an account written in the reign of Henry IV describes how pilgrims "will . . . order to have with them both men and women that can well synge wanton songes; and some other pilgremis will have with them bagge pipes, so that every toune they come throwe, what with the noyse of their singynge and with the sound of their pipyng and with the jangling of their Canterbury bellis, and with the barking out of doggis after them, they make more noise than if the kinge came there awaye with all his clarions and many other menstrelles".

Medieval bagpipes varied. Some had one or two drones in separate stocks, and others appeared to have none; some had double chanters, both with finger-holes, or one played as a drone. The chanter usually flared into a bell; in Wales, as in some other countries, the pibcorn or hornpipe (see p. 75) was tied into the bag. Some of the pipes were carved with heads of animals, and the bags had ornate covers; a piper attached to a noble or a city could carry the appropriate standard on his drone-pipe.

The origins and antiquity of the pipes are still obscure. However, it is certain that in the thirteenth century they became common in Europe, and musicians applied much skill and invention to their construction and playing. At some time just before this flowering, the idea of fitting a bag to a reed pipe and so getting a continuous and more powerful windflow spread quickly over the continent. The chief players of pipes were herdsmen and shepherds, and their application of this idea led to a variety of bagpipes, from which would develop eventually such pipes as the Great Highland, the Uillean, and the Small-pipes.

Single chanter early medieval bagpipe without drone

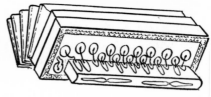

Wheatstone's Symphonium and first concertina, and an early accordion

13   THE FREE REED INSTRUMENTS

THE FREE REED INSTRUMENTS have held an honoured place among players of folk and popular music ever since they first came on to the market over a hundred years ago. They are strong and portable, and keep well in tune; they can supply folk music with the traditional drone effect to sustain the melody.

The reed is a metal tongue vibrating through an opening by means of air pressure applied by blow or suction. Pitch is determined by the length and thickness of the reed. In the harmonica (see p. 6), the reeds are arranged in pairs, one sounding on blow, the other on suck; this is known as single action. Some harmonicas have a slider stop which can switch into play a second row of reeds, tuned a semitone higher. The player has direct control over the air pressure, and can produce special effects by overblowing, a technique used in American rhythm and blues. The harmonica is not only played with great skill by such artists as Larry Adler and composed for by leading musicians, but before the last war was to be found in every schoolboy's pocket. It was played on outings and hikes, in clubs, pubs, barracks, ships, schools, and anywhere where young people got together. In some German schools there were harmonica lessons, and in America, harmonica bands. During the First World War it cheered the long marches and trench vigils on both sides of the line; British musicians organized a fund to provide harmonicas for their troops.

The German firm of Hohner, who in 1930 alone sold over forty-six million harmonicas, took up their manufacture in the middle of the last century. The first English harmonica was invented by Sir Charles Wheatstone, who also had much to do with the invention of the electric telegraph, and who was son of the House of Wheatstone, makers of musical instruments. He was interested in the new accordions coming from the Continent, and in 1829 made his symphonium, a tiny metal box enclosing twelve reeds—the first were silver, but he later used steel—operated by buttons on each side. This was also the ancestor of the concertina, patented by him in 1844.

Alone of the squeeze boxes, the concertina is not yet mass-produced here; its craftsmen makers are proud of the quality of its musical tone. The English concertina is double action (the same note on press and draw) and has a wide range of notes, divided between right- and left-hand buttons. There have been and are virtuoso players; serious music

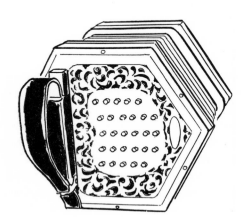

"Duet" model English concertina

The concertina at sea in the days of sail

has been composed for it, and at one time quartet instruments were made, treble, alto, tenor and bass. Small, light, and easily packed away, it has been a favourite of folk players, soldiers and sailors, and travelling showmen, and has accompanied the Salvation Army into battle.

The concertina, and the small accordion known as either a melodeon or a British or button-key chromatic accordion (see p. 10), are the most popular with folk players all over Europe. The melodeon is double action and has a right-hand button keyboard, while the left hand plays bass notes and ready made chords. The piano accordion, with a piano keyboard first added in 1852 for the right hand, and a complexity of bass notes and chords for the left, had in the thirties couplers or registers added to it, which bring in extra banks of reeds to give different effects after the manner of organ stops. In this way the players can make no end of a loud noise, which accounts for much of its popularity before the last war: sound amplification was less satisfactory then, and the piano accordion could fill a hall for dancing or accompany the community singing in vogue at the time. There were piano accordion bands, some wearing

Members of a piano accordion 'gypsy' band

Gypsy or Balkan costume in imitation of the folk players who used the accordion; the costume, like the music, was often a far cry from the original, an all-too-common feature of popped-up folk music. A gratifyingly large number of older people could not stand the row.

Folk players and Morris Men favoured the smaller accordions, and had adopted early the old models with keyed stops. Sailors, too, had taken

Morris Men with accordion

to them from the first. In the days of the square riggers they gathered during the watch preceding the long Night Watch (called the Death Watch because of the high accident rate during the small hours). Here they danced and sang, not sea shanties but "forecastle" or "deepwater" songs: long ballads, love songs, and songs of home. "There would perhaps be a man with an accordion in the middle of the hatch," wrote an American traveller, Captain Tayluer, "he would strike up a familiar tune, and away all the sailors would sing it."

The earliest accordions were made in France and Vienna, and were ornate with inlay work and painted bellows; the keys were often of ivory or mother-of-pearl. Their makers also made keyboard instru-

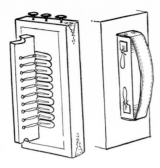

Right and left hand keys of Morris Man's accordion. The three buttons are regulators bringing in extra sets of reeds

ments with bellows operated by foot pedals or the left hand; the harmonium and the American organ, which works by suction only, developed from these; they were adopted for devotional purposes, and can still be found in churches and chapels as well as in many homes.

The principle of the free reed came to Europe in the late eighteenth century from the Far East, where for over three thousand years musicians have played a mouth-organ made from bamboos with free reeds of metal or reed. They are similar to the Cheng on page 6, the reeds remaining silent until the player closes the hole with his finger, and then producing a liquid, sweet, and unearthly note.

Early-nineteenth-century accordion

 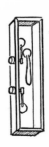

Right and left hand keys of early accordion

DRUMS AND PERCUSSION are part of orchestral, popular, jazz and brass and military band music. Pop and jazz groups use much the same percussion as the orchestra, although kettle-drums are found only in the larger ensembles. The first jazz men used for the most part second-hand army drums and percussion, and added castanets, marracas, Chinese blocks and anything that came their way: this percussion was taken into the dance bands of the twenties and thirties. Small sets of percussion could be cheaply bought for the many small bands of amateur dance musicians. The early American skiffle players made use of anything that came to hand, notably the washboard and the string bass (see p. 12), both of which were part of English skiffle during the fifties.

The orchestra too acquired its first drums and percussion from military bands; Handel scored for a pair of kettle-drums captured on the field of Dettingen. The "Turkish" percussion—long bass drum played with a knobbed stick and a switch, side-drums, kettle-drums, cymbals, triangle, Jingling Johnny and tambourine—became part of the military band during the eighteenth century. (Side- and kettle-drums were already in use for military and processional music.) Not only did the orchestra adopt this Turkish percussion, but it was borrowed for various types of light music (see p. 68) and the instruments used for general merrymaking if they were available. The Australian lagerphone of today is very like the Jingling Johnny, with bottle-tops for tintinnabula.

Apart from all this, and the toy drums and tambourines of children, there has been other percussion heard here from Anglo-Saxon times, if not earlier. One of the oldest is the tambour (Irish bureen), a single-membrane open-back drum, made from goatskin stretched over a rough wooden frame and played with a stick vibrated by the thumb. It is still

The tambour *The nakers*

played for country dancing in parts of south-west England and in Ireland. In Ireland it is played at the ancient Boxing Day custom of going round the houses and collecting for the Wren. Another is the small tabor played with the three-hole pipe, associated with morris dancing and travelling players, and also played by minstrels; it was played for dancing in gentlemen's houses as late as the eighteenth century.

The medieval nakers originated in the Middle East; they were two vessels, often made of earthenware, with skins tied over them. Like the larger kettle-drums which superseded them, they could be tuned to different notes and could provide a more interesting accompaniment to the recorder when the two were played together for dancing. They were also used for processional music, and played by wandering musicians. They were usually attached to the belt, but sometimes the player had them on the floor or a table, or strapped on to the back of an assistant.

The tambourine is now heard as a rhythm and blues instrument; like the tambour, it is of unknown antiquity. It is one of the first instruments

Pipe, tabor and timbrel, played by medieval wandering musicians and dancers

small children play in school percussion bands; as a European folk instrument it is heard in gypsy and folk music; and it is used with effect by the Salvation Army, who borrowed it from the Nigger Minstrels (see p. 26). It appears, complete with jingles, in medieval manuscripts, and was played by travelling dancers and acrobats, both men and women. The timbestere was one especially skilled with the timbrel or timbris, as it was then called, and could throw it up and catch it "ful oft Upon a fingit faire and softe" (Chaucer). The Romans used it in Bacchic rites; it was they who called the jingles the "tintinnabula".

Supplying a beat is so old and integral a part of dance music and merry-making that many other things have been used. The Nigger Minstrel bones are an old form of percussion; spoons and sticks were also clicked together in the same way. Tools of the trade were used at the ceremonies and feasts of Trade Guilds. The sweeps of London, for instance, held their May Day procession well into the last century, beating their shovels

Marrowbones and cleavers

with their brushes; the butchers beat their cleavers with marrow-bones on festive occasions, such as the wedding of a member of their fraternity. Tongs and bones were used for rhythm ("I have a reasonable good ear for music; let's have the tongs and bones," says Bottom in *A Midsummer Night's Dream*). So were bellows and tongs, and other domestic things, especially the old wooden salt-boxes, with their hinged lids, which hung beside the kitchen fire; these made no end of "clattering and battering and clapping" when shaken and beaten with the rolling-pin.

93

Spoons, bellows and tongs, and saltbox and rolling pin

The saw

15

PASSING FASHIONS

SOME INSTRUMENTS HAVE had frequent waves of popularity, while others, because of their limited performance, have had their day, or like the saw have been returned to their proper use. In between the wars, there was a fashion for playing the saw, bending back the blade and knocking it with a stick, or bowing the non-serrated edge with a violin bow; the second way wore out the horse-hair, but produced an unearthly echoing sound of the sort now associated with Outer Space music. Not unlike was the sound of the nail violin invented around 1750; this too was played with a fiddle bow, the longer nails producing the lower notes.

A ghostly sounding instrument was the Aeolian harp; this was a box strung with wire strings of different weights, which was hung in a tree

Eighteenth-century nail violin (sometimes two bows were used)

or in some place where the wind could sound the strings, and play, as an eighteenth-century poet put it, "such sweet, such sad, such solemn Airs divine". This was popular during the "Romantic" periods between 1750 and 1850, when fashionable people had crazes for such things as ruined temples, haunted castles, horror stories, and simple "rustic" life. (By contrast, this period also saw the coming of steam power and the rise of modern industry.)

Another romantic instrument was the glass harmonica, with its weird sounds seeming to come from infinity and fading away into it. In 1761 Benjamin Franklin from America made it in its final form with graduated glass bowls on a spindle turned by a foot pedal; as it turned, the rims dipped into water, and were sounded by the fingers. There was a fashion for this; several composers wrote music for it, and there were a number of virtuoso players. However, the effect of the high lingering harmonics and the friction of the wet glass tended to drive its players mad, and they had to give up. Mechanical devices robbed it of its peculiar and seductive tones.

Leading up to Franklin's invention were the musical glasses, tuned by sizes and different water levels. Gluck had composed for "Twenty-six Drinking Glasses, tuned with Spring Water", and in 1823 a Mr. Edwards performed on a set of over 120, from a three gallon size to that of a thimble; while a writer in 1677 mentions "gay wine music".

The Aeolian harp

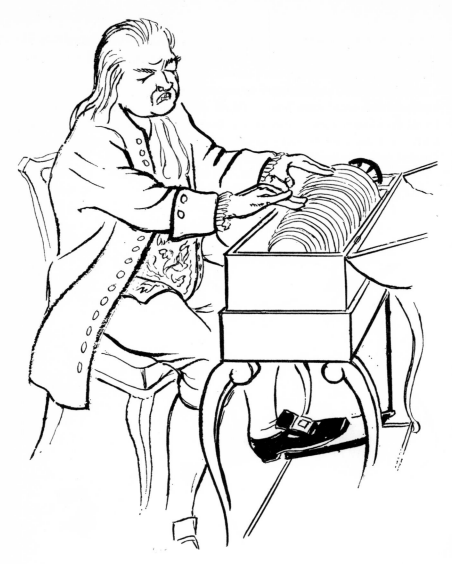

The glass harmonica

The kazoo is a mirliton, an instrument which alters and amplifies the voice when a membrane such as skin or paper is sung against; comb and paper is a mirliton. The kazoo, now sold as a toy, is also played in some industrial areas in processional music provided by the drum and kazoo bands, which were started in South Wales during the General Strike of 1926. It was brought to England at that time by the Mound City Blue Blowers skiffle players, and was one of the early skiffle instruments in the United States.

There was, however, a rather similar toy in Victorian times, the Zahzah, or voice flute. (The holes are fingered as for a trill to produce a *tremolo*.) This was practically the same as the Eunuch flute illustrated in Mersennes '*Harmonie Universalle*' of 1637.

membrane

The zahzah and the kazoo

Eighteenth-century hurdy-gurdy

English dulcimer

16   OTHER FOLK INSTRUMENTS

THERE ARE A NUMBER of instruments now played for folk music that have recently come to this country, while there are others, such as the pibcorn and the rebec, which have become obsolete. Such an instrument is the hurdy-gurdy or rota. In Europe this was not only a popular folk instrument—and still is in some parts—but was played by all classes and had some music composed for it. It was less common in Britain, being played occasionally as a street instrument early last century, and as a folk instrument before that; it figures in some of the church carvings of minstrels. The strings are sounded by a wheel turned by the handle; it has two melody strings stopped by tangents operated by a keyboard, and two bourdon strings that can be adjusted to play all the time; sometimes there are also thin wire "sympathetic" strings, unplayed but vibrating in sympathy with the others; it thus provided a good loud melody and sustaining drone for folk dancing. It originated as early as A.D. 1000 in Church music, called an organistrum, a large instrument that took two players, one to turn and one to press the keys.

An instrument still played by a very few folk musicians is the English dulcimer. This has courses of three or four wire strings across a shallow box, and is plucked, or more often beaten with cane beaters. It can be played very rapidly, and the way in which the harmonics continue to sound (there is no damper mechanism as in the piano) and underlie the *staccato* melody gives an unusual drone effect. Although it has rarely been played in Britain since the seventeenth century, similar dulcimers are popular Eastern European folk instruments. Its ancestor is the medieval psaltery (see p. 9) seen in so many representations of angelic music, and widespread during the fifteenth and fourteenth centuries; its sound was more harplike, being played with a quill.

A very old instrument, in many parts of the world, is the Jews'

Jews' Harp or guimbarde

Harp. The metal tongue is vibrated, and the mouth acts as a resonator; it is possible, by changing the shape of the mouth, to obtain a few harmonic notes of a deep twanging nature. Never an instrument of serious music, and now little more than a toy, it has appeared in history in very differing situations. There were, about 150 years ago, virtuoso players who managed two at a time, or several in succession; in the eighteenth and seventeenth centuries in Scotland it was played for some folk dancing, as it still is in parts of Sicily, with a strong rhythm, and a carrying power that one would think impossible; in Scotland, too, called the trump, it was played for the ritual dancing of the Old Religion, and it has a long connection with magic and courtship customs. Yet it appears among the carved minstrels in some churches, and also on the crozier of a medieval archbishop. Although the smallest, it is one of the most mysterious of instruments.

The folk revival has brought new instruments to this country as yet played only by a few. One coming from America, and first made in nineteenth-century Germany, is the autoharp; this provides sweeping harp-like chords, some of which can be cut out by dampers; it is used to accompany folk singing. Another is the Appalachian or mountain dulcimer, descendant of rather similar Scandinavian folk instruments. This is finger plucked, having one fretted melody string stopped with a small stick, and two bourdons; its gentle clear notes are evocative of the lullabies and farewells that are part of folk tradition. A third is the

Appalachian dulcimer   *Autoharp*

picking or mouth bow from Africa; it can be plucked or hit, and the resonance is provided by the mouth or a tin resonator. It is a primitive
instrument that takes us to the dawn of musical instrumentation. No one
knows whether it was the first instrument of all, but it is the first as yet
known to have been portrayed by the hand of man: among the paintings
of animals in the cave of Les Trois Frères in France (paintings which may
be thirty thousand years old) is the figure of a man dressed in an animal
skin and playing a mouth bow.

Mouth and picking bows

Short Bibliography

Books readily available at booksellers and libraries:
GROVE, *Dictionary of Music and Musicians.* Macmillan.
SCHOLES, *Oxford Companion to Music.* Oxford University Press.
Musical Instruments Through the Ages, ed. A. BAINES, a Pelican Book.
HARRISON AND RIMMER, *European Musical Instruments,* Studio Vista, London.
A. BAINES, *Woodwind Instruments and their History.* Faber.

Books which can be obtained through your Public Library:
BESSARABOFF, NICHOLAS, *Ancient European Musical Instruments.* Harvard Press.
BRINSMEAD, EDGAR, *History of the Pianoforte.* Cassell.
CARSE, ADAM, *Musical Wind Instruments.* Da Capo Press.
CHAPELL, WILLIAM, *Popular Music of the Olden Time.* Chapell.
ENGEL, CARL, *Musical Instruments.* Chapman & Hall.
GALPIN, F. W., *Old English Instruments of Music.* Methuen.
Galpin Society Journal, first issued in 1948. Galpin Society.
KINSKY, GEORG, *History of Music in Pictures.* Dent.
PANUM, HORTENSE, *The Stringed Instruments of the Middle Ages.* Reeves.
SACHS, CURT, *The History of Musical Instruments.* Naughton, N.Y.
WELCH, CHRISTOPHER, *Six Lectures on the Recorder.* Frowde.

Appendix

THE SCALES

The Diatonic scale is the division of the octave into eight notes, making the major and minor scales upon which most Western music is based.

Diatonic scale of G Major.

The Chromatic scale divides the octave into thirteen semitones.
Chromatic scale of G.

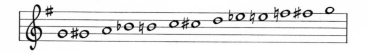

The Harmonic scale is made up of the harmonics, or overtones, of the Tonic or key-note. The harmonics of any note are heard simultaneously, but certain instruments give greater or lesser value to some of them. Other instruments, e.g. the bugle, can produce the harmonics separately; bugle calls are made up of these notes, which are obtained by methods of blowing.
Harmonic scale of G.

Glossary

Bourdon: an open string sounding a drone throughout a theme played on the other strings.

Counterpoint: the harmonious interweaving of two or more independent themes.

Crescendo: gradually becoming louder.

Diminuendo: gradually becoming softer.

Drone: a single note sustained throughout a theme: a pipe or string for this purpose.

Glissando: sliding from one note to another.

Legato: smoothly.

Obbligato: an instrumental part, often a solo, necessary for the effect of the whole; often used to mean an extra part or instrumental accompaniment to the voice.

Staccato: each note clearly detached.

Stop (n): a device used to alter tone by bringing in extra ranks of pipes on organs, and by bringing in extra strings on harpsichords and also controlling the place in which the strings are plucked.

Stop (v.a.): to close hole or depress key on wind instruments; to shorten vibrating length of string by pressure of finger or tangent.

Trill: an ornament consisting of adjacent notes repeated alternately.

Vibrato: fluctuation of pitch caused by varying means to make a noticeable vibration in the sound.

Virtuoso: highly skilled in the execution of difficult or showy passages.

Organizations useful to the student

(When writing inquiries, enclose S.A.E.)

The British Institute of Recorded Sound (national collection of sound recordings): lectures, recitals, information, library.
38 Russell Square. W.C.1.

The Dolmetsch Foundation: concerts and recitals, information; fifteenth to eighteenth-century instruments.
Greeenstead, Beacon Hill, Hindhead, Surrey.

The English Folk Dance and Song Society: information on all Folk Dance and Song activities, festivals, groups, etc; recordings, library.
Cecil Sharp House, 2 Regent's Park Rd, N.W.1.

The Galpin Society: information on the history of musical instruments; lectures, recitals, demonstrations.
Sec. Jeremy Montague, 7, Pickwick Rd, S.E.21.

Musica Reservata: medieval and Renaissance instruments and music; concerts, lectures, demonstrations.
Sec. Michael Morrow, 9 Aberdare Gardens, N.W. 6.

Northumbrian Pipers' Society:
Sec. Forster Charlton, 135 Sidney Grove. Newcastle 4.

Museums

THE HORNIMAN MUSEUM, Forest Hill, S.E. 23 (*closed on Monday*).

THE VICTORIA AND ALBERT MUSEUM, Kensington, S.W.7.

THE PITT RIVERS MUSEUM, Oxford (*2–4 only*).

BRIGHTON MUNICIPAL MUSEUM (*the Spencer Collection*).

FOLK MUSEUM, Cambridge.

LUTON BOROUGH MUSEUM (*the Ridley Collection of wind instruments*).

CASTLE MUSEUM, York.

THE ROYAL SCOTTISH MUSEUM, Edinburgh.

THE WELSH FOLK MUSEUM, St. Fagans Castle, Cardiff.

Most local museums and Stately Homes on view to the public have instruments among their collections.

COLLECTIONS can be seen in the following establishments:

FENTON HOUSE, Hampstead, N.W.3 (*keyboard instruments*).

GLEN, Bagpipe maker, Edinburgh.

REUBEN GREEN, Hinton Rd, S.E.24 (*by arrangement only*).

S. COLT, Bethusden, in Ashford, Kent (*keyboard instruments by appointment only*).

PAYTON'S MUSIC STORES, Islington High St. N.1.

THE REID SCHOOL OF MUSIC. Edinburgh.

THE ROYAL COLLEGE OF MUSIC, Kensington, S.W.7 (*the Donaldson Collection, termtime only*).

RUSHWORTH AND DREAPER, Music dealers, Liverpool.

Index

INDEX

INSTRUMENTS OF POPULAR MUSIC